QUANTUM HEALING CODES

The Science Language of Wellness

By

Ecnal Ver

Contents

Suggestion for Reading

Skip to the back of the book and read the **Glossary of Terms** and the **Codes List**. A quick review of this information will assist you in getting a fuller understanding of what you read.

Introduction The Language of Quantum Healing Codes

Imagine a world where health and healing are no longer limited by physical boundaries. A world where your body, mind, and spirit can align with universal energies to activate your innate potential for self-healing.

This is the essence of **Quantum Healing Codes**—a groundbreaking system of energetic patterns that bridge ancient wisdom and cutting-edge quantum science to unlock new possibilities for wellness.

Throughout history, humanity has sought ways to understand the intricate relationship between energy, matter, and health. From sacred geometric patterns to harmonic sound frequencies, ancient civilizations intuited that the universe operates through a language of energy.

Today, quantum physics confirms what mystics and healers have long known: we are not just physical beings; we are energetic beings living within a field of infinite potential. **Quantum Healing Codes** are the keys to accessing this potential, offering a transformative path to balance, harmony, and vitality.

What Are Quantum Healing Codes?

At their core, quantum healing codes are energetic signatures designed to communicate with the quantum field—the invisible web of energy that connects all things.

1

These codes function like passwords, unlocking pathways for healing at the deepest levels.

Each code resonates with a specific frequency that aligns with the body's natural rhythms, promoting restoration and renewal. Whether through sound, light, visualization, or intention, these codes have the power to recalibrate your energy field and harmonize your physical, emotional, and spiritual states.

The concept of codes may seem abstract, but think of them as the universe's programming language. Just as computer code drives the function of modern technology, quantum healing codes drive energetic transformation.

By learning how to activate and apply these codes, you can rewrite old patterns of illness, stress, or imbalance and replace them with vibrant health and well-being.

The Quantum Blueprint for Healing

Quantum science has shown us that everything in existence vibrates at its unique frequency, including our bodies. When these frequencies are disrupted—whether by trauma, illness, or environmental factors—imbalance and disease can manifest.

Quantum healing codes work by restoring coherence to these vibrations, aligning the body's energetic blueprint with the natural rhythms of the universe.

Unlike conventional approaches to healing, which often treat symptoms rather than root causes, quantum healing codes operate at the foundational level of energy. They tap into the quantum field's limitless potential, offering an opportunity for healing that transcends physical boundaries.

This approach is not limited to curing disease; it's about fostering holistic harmony in your life, from emotional resilience to spiritual awakening.

Bridging Science and Spirituality

The beauty of quantum healing codes lies in their ability to unite two seemingly different worlds: science and spirituality. Quantum physics teaches us that particles can exist in multiple states, that observation influences reality, and that all things are interconnected.

These principles are not merely theoretical; they form the basis of how quantum healing codes function. By applying focused intention and resonance, you can influence your energetic state and create a ripple effect of positive change.

On the spiritual side, quantum healing codes resonate with ancient practices that honor the unseen forces shaping our lives. Indigenous cultures, Eastern philosophies, and mystical traditions have long recognized the power of energy, sound, and symbols as tools for healing.

Quantum healing codes draw from this wisdom while integrating modern scientific insights, making them accessible and effective for today's world.

How This Book Will Guide You

This book is your comprehensive guide to understanding, activating, and applying quantum healing codes in your life. Whether you're new to the concept of energy healing or have years of experience, the insights and practices within these pages will empower you to take charge of your health in ways you never thought possible.

Discover the Foundations: Learn the science behind quantum healing and the origins of healing codes.

- Activate the Codes: Explore practical techniques to unlock the power of healing codes, from sound therapy to visualization exercises.
- Transform Your Life: Apply codes to address specific areas of healing, including physical ailments, emotional blocks, and spiritual growth.
- Create Your Own Codes: Harness your intuition to design personalized codes tailored to your unique needs.

Each chapter builds upon the last, taking you on a journey from understanding the principles of quantum healing to mastering the art of creating and using your codes. By the end of this book, you'll have a powerful toolkit to support your health and well-being, as well as the confidence to share this knowledge with others.

An Invitation to Heal

As you embark on this journey, we invite you to open your mind and heart to the infinite possibilities of the quantum field. Healing is not a one-size-fits-all process; it's a deeply personal and dynamic experience. With **Quantum Healing Codes**, you have the tools to reconnect with your true essence, restore balance, and unlock your body's incredible capacity for self-healing.

This book is more than a guide—it's an invitation to step into a new paradigm of health. A paradigm where you are an active participant in your healing journey, co-creating your reality with the universe. The codes are waiting. The potential is within you.

Let's begin.

ECNAL VER

CH 1 The Origins of Quantum Healing Codes

The concept of quantum healing codes, though modern in its terminology, is rooted in an amalgamation of ancient wisdom and cutting-edge scientific discovery. These codes represent energetic patterns or frequencies designed to unlock the body's innate ability to heal and regenerate.

Understanding their origins allows us to appreciate the profound interplay between the spiritual and scientific realms that birthed this revolutionary approach to healing.

Ancient Wisdom and Healing Patterns

Long before the advent of modern medicine, ancient civilizations relied on energy-based healing practices. From the sacred geometry of the Egyptians to the mantras of Indian Vedic traditions, the idea that energy holds the key to health and harmony has always been present.

These practices often involved specific patterns, sounds, or symbols believed to resonate with the body's natural frequencies, aligning the individual with the greater universal energy.

For instance, the Flower of Life, a geometric pattern found in various ancient cultures, is thought to contain the blueprint of creation itself. Similarly, the solfeggio frequencies, a set of sacred sound vibrations, were used in Gregorian chants to invoke healing and spiritual alignment.

These ancient tools can be seen as the precursors to modern quantum healing codes, offering a glimpse into humanity's long-standing recognition of energy's healing potential.

The Quantum Revolution

The 20th century brought about a profound shift in how we understand the universe. With the advent of quantum mechanics, scientists began to uncover the invisible forces that govern matter and energy.

At its core, quantum theory reveals that everything in the universe, including the human body, is composed of vibrating energy fields. This understanding laid the foundation for the development of quantum healing codes.

One of the most groundbreaking discoveries in quantum physics is the concept of wave-particle duality, which demonstrates that particles can behave as both solid matter and waves of energy.

This dual nature underscores the interconnectedness of all things, suggesting that the human body is not merely a physical entity but also a dynamic field of energy that can be influenced by external frequencies.

Bridging Ancient and Modern

Quantum healing codes serve as a bridge between ancient wisdom and modern science. They leverage the timeless understanding of energy's role in health while incorporating the precision of quantum mechanics.

By decoding and harnessing specific frequencies, these codes provide a targeted approach to healing that aligns with the body's energetic blueprint.

The codes themselves are derived from a combination of principles, including sacred geometry, sound vibrations, and quantum field theory. They are designed to resonate with the body's natural frequencies, promoting balance and harmony.

For example, a healing code might be based on the Fibonacci sequence, a mathematical pattern found throughout nature, or a specific sound frequency known to influence cellular regeneration.

The Body as an Energy System

To fully grasp the power of quantum healing codes, it's essential to understand the human body as an energy system. Ancient traditions such as Traditional Chinese Medicine (TCM) and Ayurveda have long recognized the existence of energy pathways, known as meridians or nadis, which flow through the body.

Blockages or imbalances in these pathways are believed to lead to illness, while restoring their flow can promote healing.

Quantum healing codes operate on a similar principle, targeting the body's energetic pathways to remove blockages and restore balance. They work by interacting with the body's biofield, a complex system of electromagnetic energy that surrounds and interpenetrates the physical body.

This biofield serves as the interface between the physical and energetic aspects of a person, making it the ideal medium for the application of healing codes.

The Role of Intention and Consciousness

One of the most intriguing aspects of quantum healing codes is their reliance on intention and consciousness. In quantum mechanics, the observer effect demonstrates that the act of observation can influence the behavior of particles.

This principle suggests that human consciousness plays a direct role in shaping reality, including the body's ability to heal.

When using quantum healing codes, intention acts as the catalyst that activates their power. By focusing on a specific healing outcome, individuals can amplify the effects of the codes, directing their energy toward the desired result.

This intentionality aligns with practices such as prayer and meditation, which have long been associated with healing.

Codes as Universal Blueprints

Quantum healing codes can be thought of as universal blueprints for health and harmony. Just as DNA contains the instructions for building and maintaining the body, healing codes provide the energetic instructions for restoring balance and vitality.

These codes tap into the quantum field, a vast reservoir of energy and information that connects all things, to retrieve the frequencies needed for healing.

Each code is unique, designed to address a specific aspect of health or well-being. Some codes may target physical conditions, such as reducing inflammation or accelerating tissue repair, while others may focus on emotional or spiritual healing, such as releasing trauma or enhancing intuition.

By aligning with these codes, individuals can access the quantum field's unlimited potential to facilitate transformation.

Real-World Applications of Quantum Healing Codes

The practical applications of quantum healing codes are as diverse as the codes themselves. They can be used in a variety of settings, from self-healing practices to professional energy healing sessions. Common methods of applying the codes include:

- **Visualization**: Focusing on the code's pattern or symbol while meditating.
- **Sound Therapy**: Listening to frequencies associated with the code.
- **Light Therapy**: Using colors or light patterns that correspond to the code's vibration.
- **Energy Work**: Incorporating the codes into modalities such as Reiki or acupuncture.

These techniques allow individuals to integrate quantum healing codes into their daily lives, empowering them to take an active role in their health and well-being.

The Future of Healing

As the understanding of quantum healing codes continues to evolve, their potential for transforming healthcare becomes increasingly apparent. By addressing the root causes of illness at the energetic level, these codes offer a holistic approach to healing that complements traditional medical treatments.

They also hold promise for preventive care, enabling individuals to maintain optimal health by harmonizing their energy fields.

In addition to their individual applications, quantum healing codes have the potential to create a ripple effect of healing on a collective scale.

By raising the vibrational frequency of individuals, these codes can contribute to a broader shift toward health and harmony within communities and the world at large.

Energy is the Foundation

The origins of quantum healing codes lie in the timeless understanding that energy is the foundation of all existence. By merging ancient wisdom with modern science, these codes provide a powerful tool for unlocking the body's innate healing potential.

As we continue to explore their possibilities, quantum healing codes offer a pathway to a future where health and vitality are accessible to all.

ECNAL VER

CH 2 The Science Behind the Codes

The universe operates on principles that are both profound and intricate, with quantum physics offering a glimpse into the underlying fabric of reality.

At its core, quantum healing codes derive their power from this quantum realm—a space where particles can exist in multiple states simultaneously, where energy fields interconnect, and where intention and observation influence outcomes.

To truly understand how these codes function, it is essential to explore the science that supports them.

The Quantum World and Energy Fields

Quantum mechanics teaches us that everything in the universe, including the human body, is made of energy. At a microscopic level, particles that form matter are not solid but are instead vibrational energy fields.

These fields are dynamic, constantly interacting with the environment, and are influenced by factors such as thoughts, emotions, and external stimuli.

Healing codes operate within these energy fields, working as vibrational "keys" that align and harmonize disordered or imbalanced energy. By targeting specific frequencies, these codes influence the body's natural ability to heal itself. This aligns with the principle of resonance, where matching frequencies amplify each other, creating a harmonious state.

Resonance and Healing Frequencies

Resonance is the phenomenon where an object vibrating at a specific frequency causes another object with the same natural frequency to vibrate. For example, a tuning fork struck in a room can cause another tuning fork of the same frequency to resonate.

Similarly, the human body, as an intricate system of energy and vibrations, can respond to external frequencies, including healing codes.

Quantum healing codes are essentially vibrational patterns that resonate with specific aspects of the body, mind, or spirit. For example:

- A code for emotional healing may resonate with the heart chakra, easing feelings of grief or fear.
- A physical healing code might target cellular vibrations, encouraging regeneration and repair.
- A spiritual awakening code could align with higher frequencies, opening pathways to deeper intuition and consciousness.

By introducing these codes into an energy field, they recalibrate and restore balance, much like how a musical instrument is tuned to produce harmonious sound.

Wave-Particle Duality and Intentionality

One of the most fascinating aspects of quantum mechanics is the concept of wave-particle duality. Subatomic particles, such as electrons, exhibit both wave-like and particle-like behavior, depending on how they are observed.

This suggests that the act of observation or intention has a direct influence on the behavior of energy at the quantum level.

In the context of quantum healing codes, intention plays a critical role. When a person uses a code with focused intent, they act as the observer, directing energy to manifest a desired outcome.

For example, reciting or visualizing a healing code with the intention of relieving pain can amplify its effectiveness. The observer's intention essentially "collapses" the quantum field into a state that promotes healing.

Coherence and the Power of Alignment

Coherence is another key concept in quantum science. It refers to the state where waves are synchronized, moving in harmony to create a unified and powerful effect.

In biological systems, coherence is observed in the rhythms of the heart, brain, and other physiological processes when the body is in a state of balance.

Quantum healing codes work to establish coherence within the body's energy systems. For instance:

- A disrupted energy field, often caused by stress, trauma, or illness, exhibits chaotic patterns.
- Healing codes introduce vibrational frequencies that synchronize these patterns, restoring harmony.
- This coherence supports the body's natural healing mechanisms, enhancing physical and emotional well-being.

Scientific research into heart coherence, such as studies conducted by the HeartMath Institute, highlights how specific frequencies and intentional practices can synchronize heart rhythms, reduce stress, and improve overall health. Healing codes align with these findings, acting as tools to foster coherence at a quantum level.

The Role of Quantum Entanglement

Quantum entanglement is a phenomenon where particles become interconnected, such that the state of one particle instantly influences the state of another, regardless of distance.

This concept supports the idea of non-locality, where energy and information are not confined to a single location but are shared across the quantum field.

Healing codes leverage this principle of entanglement. When a code is activated—through visualization, sound, or intention—it resonates not only within the individual using it but also within the broader energy field.

This allows for distant healing, where codes can influence others regardless of physical proximity. For example, a practitioner might use a code to send healing vibrations to a loved one miles away, with the entangled energy facilitating the transfer.

The Biology of Energy and Cellular Response

At the cellular level, the body responds to energy vibrations in profound ways. Cells communicate through bioelectrical signals, and disruptions in this communication can lead to illness.

Quantum healing codes interact with these cellular signals, helping to restore proper communication pathways.

For instance:

- Cells are surrounded by a plasma membrane, which acts as a barrier and a gateway for signals.
- Healing codes, through their specific frequencies, influence these membranes, promoting optimal cellular function.
- This can enhance processes such as nutrient absorption, toxin elimination, and DNA repair.

Additionally, research into biophotons—light particles emitted by cells—suggests that cells use light to communicate.

Healing codes, particularly those incorporating light frequencies, may amplify this biophotonic communication, enhancing the body's natural healing processes.

The Placebo Effect and Belief Systems

The placebo effect is a well-documented phenomenon where belief in a treatment's effectiveness leads to real physiological improvements, even when the treatment itself is inert. This highlights the power of the mind in influencing the body's healing processes.

Quantum healing codes integrate the placebo effect by fostering a strong belief in their power. When a person trusts in the efficacy of a code, their subconscious mind aligns with the healing intention, amplifying the code's impact.

This synergy between belief and quantum science underscores the importance of mental and emotional states in the healing journey.

Practical Applications of the Science

Understanding the science behind quantum healing codes empowers individuals to use them more effectively. Here are practical steps to harness their potential:

Set Clear Intentions: Focus your mind on the specific healing outcome you desire. Visualize the code as a vibrational key unlocking your energy field.

Engage the Senses: Combine the code with sound (e.g., chanting) or light (e.g., visualization of colors) to enhance its resonance.

Practice Regularly: Repetition strengthens the connection between the code and your energy field, making it more effective over time.

Cultivate Belief: Trust in the process. Belief amplifies the power of the codes by aligning your conscious and subconscious mind with the healing intention.

Bridging Science and Spirituality

Quantum healing codes represent a bridge between science and spirituality, merging the empirical principles of quantum physics with the intuitive wisdom of energy medicine.

While science provides the framework for understanding how codes function, spirituality invites us to trust in the unseen forces that guide and heal us.

This union of science and spirituality offers a holistic approach to health and well-being, empowering individuals to take an active role in their healing journey.

By tapping into the quantum realm, healing codes open the door to infinite possibilities, reminding us that the universe's most profound truths often lie beyond the physical.

In this chapter, we've explored the fascinating scientific principles that underpin quantum healing codes, from resonance and coherence to entanglement and cellular response.

As we delve deeper into subsequent chapters, we'll uncover the specific codes and practices that bring these principles to life, guiding readers toward their own quantum healing transformation.

ECNAL VER

CH 3 Decoding Your Energetic Blueprint

The concept of an energetic blueprint is rooted in the understanding that every individual has a unique vibrational signature that reflects their physical, emotional, and spiritual health.

In the realm of **Quantum Healing Codes**, this blueprint serves as the foundation for identifying areas of imbalance and aligning them with frequencies that promote healing and harmony.

This chapter delves into how to recognize and interpret your energetic blueprint and introduces tools and techniques to decode and recalibrate it using quantum healing codes.

What is an Energetic Blueprint?

At its core, the energetic blueprint is a map of your personal energy field. It includes the subtle frequencies that govern your health, emotions, and spiritual connection.

Just as DNA encodes physical traits, your energetic blueprint encodes the vibrational patterns that influence how you experience life. This invisible framework is constantly interacting with the world around you, shaping your responses to stress, relationships, and even physical ailments.

When your energetic blueprint is in balance, you feel vibrant, connected, and at peace. However, disruptions in this blueprint can manifest as physical pain, emotional distress, or spiritual disconnection.

The role of **Quantum Healing Codes** is to identify these disruptions and restore coherence to your energy field.

Understanding Imbalances in the Blueprint

Imbalances in your energetic blueprint often stem from various sources:

Physical Stressors: Illness, injury, or environmental toxins can disrupt the flow of energy in your body.

Emotional Trauma: Past experiences of grief, fear, or anger can create energetic blockages that persist over time.

Negative Thought Patterns: Chronic negative thinking or limiting beliefs can lower your vibrational frequency.

Spiritual Disconnect: A lack of alignment with your higher purpose or inner self can leave your energy field fragmented.

These imbalances show up in specific ways, such as recurring health issues, emotional instability, or feelings of being "stuck." Recognizing these patterns is the first step toward healing.

How Quantum Healing Codes Interact with the Blueprint

Quantum healing codes are energetic frequencies encoded in symbols, sounds, or visualizations that resonate with specific aspects of your blueprint.

When applied intentionally, these codes act as tuning forks, recalibrating your vibrational field and restoring harmony. Each code corresponds to a particular energy frequency, targeting areas of imbalance and activating the body's natural healing mechanisms.

For instance:

- A code for **physical healing** might align with the frequency of cellular regeneration.
- A code for **emotional release** could resonate with forgiveness and letting go of past pain.
- A code for **spiritual connection** might enhance intuition and align you with your higher self.

The interaction between your energetic blueprint and the codes is dynamic, meaning the same code can have different effects depending on your unique vibrational needs.

Tools for Decoding Your Energetic Blueprint

Decoding your energetic blueprint involves identifying areas of imbalance and understanding their root causes. Below are some practical tools and techniques to help you uncover the state of your energy field:

Body Awareness

Pay attention to areas of tension, discomfort, or pain in your body. These physical sensations often correlate with energetic blockages.

Use a body scan meditation to identify regions where energy feels heavy or stagnant.

Emotional Reflection

Reflect on recurring emotions that dominate your daily life. Are you often anxious, angry, or sad? These emotions can point to imbalances in your emotional energy field.

Journaling can help you uncover patterns and triggers that contribute to these emotions.

Chakra Analysis

The chakra system is a powerful framework for assessing your energy field. Imbalances in specific chakras often correspond to physical, emotional, or spiritual issues.

Tools like pendulums or chakra cards can help you pinpoint which chakras need attention.

Intuitive Sensing

Your intuition is a valuable guide in understanding your energetic blueprint. Practice tuning into your gut feelings and inner knowing to gain insights into your energy field.

Techniques like automatic writing or guided visualization can enhance your intuitive abilities.

Energy Testing

Muscle testing (also known as applied kinesiology) is a simple yet effective method for identifying energetic imbalances. By testing the strength of a muscle in response to a specific question or stimulus, you can uncover hidden energetic disruptions.

Aligning Codes with Your Blueprint

Once you've identified areas of imbalance, the next step is to align the appropriate quantum healing codes with your energetic blueprint. Here's how:

Set Your Intention

Healing begins with clear intention. Focus on the area you wish to address, whether it's physical pain, emotional healing, or spiritual growth.

Example: "I intend to release the emotional pain stored in my heart chakra and restore balance to my energy field."

Choose the Right Code

Select a quantum healing code that resonates with your intention. Codes can be represented as symbols, mantras, or sound frequencies.

Example: A symbol for emotional healing might resemble a flowing wave, signifying the release of stuck energy.

Activate the Code

Visualization: Imagine the code entering your energy field and radiating its frequency throughout your body.

Chanting: Repeat a sound or mantra associated with the code to amplify its effect.

Meditation: Sit quietly with the code in mind, allowing its energy to permeate your awareness.

Observe and Adjust

Notice how your energy shifts after activating the code. You may feel lighter, more grounded, or emotionally released.

If a code doesn't resonate, try another one or adjust your intention to match your current needs.

Practical Exercises for Decoding and Healing

To make this process accessible, here are a few exercises you can start with:

Energy Blueprint Mapping

Take a few minutes to sit in a quiet space and visualize your body's energy field.

Imagine scanning your body with a gentle light, noting areas where the light feels dim or blocked.

Record your observations in a journal.

Healing with Sound

Use tuning forks or listen to solfeggio frequencies to align your energy field.

Focus on one area of imbalance at a time, allowing the sound to wash over that part of your body.

Chakra Balancing Visualization

Visualize each chakra as a spinning wheel of light.

Imagine infusing each chakra with a quantum healing code, represented as a unique color or shape.

Feel the energy flow harmoniously through your entire body.

The Role of Self-Awareness

Decoding your energetic blueprint is an ongoing journey that requires self-awareness and patience. As you become more attuned to your energy field, you'll notice subtle shifts and patterns that guide your healing process.

Over time, you'll develop a deeper understanding of how quantum healing codes interact with your blueprint and how to use them effectively.

Remember, your energetic blueprint is not static—it evolves with your experiences, thoughts, and intentions. By maintaining a practice of self-reflection and energy alignment, you can ensure that your blueprint remains a vibrant and accurate reflection of your true self.

A New Way Forward

Decoding your energetic blueprint is not just about addressing imbalances—it's about reclaiming your power to create a life of health, harmony, and purpose. By understanding your unique vibrational signature and learning to align it with the transformative power of

Quantum Healing Codes, you open the door to a new paradigm of healing.

With each step, you are rewriting the energetic story of your life, one code at a time.

CH 4 The Core
Healing Codes

Quantum Healing Codes are the foundational tools in the art of quantum-based transformation. These codes, derived from universal frequencies, act as energetic blueprints that help the body, mind, and spirit align with their natural state of health and balance.

This chapter explores the core quantum healing codes, their purpose, and how to activate them for optimal results.

What Are Core Healing Codes?

Core healing codes are the primary frequencies that resonate with the universal energies of health, harmony, and vitality. They are designed to recalibrate the energetic systems of the body, facilitating healing on physical, emotional, and spiritual levels.

Each code is a vibrational signature, like a unique "song" that resonates with specific aspects of the human experience.

For instance, there are codes that target stress reduction, cellular regeneration, emotional release, and spiritual awakening. These codes can be visualized as patterns, numbers, or tones, depending on the user's preference and intuitive connection.

Understanding the Universal Frequencies

Core healing codes are grounded in the concept of universal frequencies, which are vibrations that govern all matter and energy.

These include:

Love (528 Hz): The frequency associated with unconditional love and cellular repair. Often referred to as the "miracle tone," it is believed to promote DNA healing and restore harmony in the body.

Harmony (432 Hz): A natural frequency found in nature, this code aligns the mind and spirit, fostering balance and inner peace.

Gratitude (741 Hz): This frequency is linked to emotional release, detoxification, and freeing the mind from negativity.

These universal frequencies act as the building blocks of the core healing codes, each one carrying a specific purpose and resonance.

Core Healing Codes and Their Functions

Below are some of the most impactful core healing codes, along with their primary functions:

Code of Vitality

- Frequency: 285 Hz

- Purpose: Cellular regeneration and physical healing.

- Application: Use this code when experiencing fatigue, physical pain, or recovery from illness. It works to restore energy flow and repair damaged tissues.

Code of Emotional Release

- Frequency: 396 Hz

- Purpose: Liberates the user from fear, guilt, and shame.

- Application: Ideal for those processing emotional trauma or seeking emotional clarity. It helps dissolve negative patterns and restore a sense of peace.

Code of Intuition

- Frequency: 639 Hz

- Purpose: Enhances connection with oneself and others.

- Application: This code is helpful for strengthening relationships, fostering empathy, and opening the heart chakra.

Code of Divine Connection

- Frequency: 852 Hz

- Purpose: Awakens spiritual awareness and connects with higher consciousness.

- Application: Use during meditation or spiritual practice to deepen your sense of connection with the universe.

Activating the Healing Codes

The power of quantum healing codes lies in their activation. These codes are not passive; they require intentional engagement to become effective. Below are methods to activate the core healing codes:

Visualization

- Imagine the code as a luminous, vibrating symbol. Visualize it entering your energy field, harmonizing with your body, and flowing through your chakras.

- For example, when using the Code of Vitality (285 Hz), picture a golden light repairing cells and energizing your body.

Sound Frequencies

- Each code has a corresponding sound frequency. Listening to these tones through meditative music or frequency generators helps attune your body to the desired vibration.

- Use headphones for a more immersive experience, allowing the sound to wash over you and create resonance.

Affirmations

Combine the codes with affirmations to amplify their power. For instance, while using the Code of Gratitude (741 Hz), repeat: "I release all negativity and embrace the purity of gratitude."

Symbols and Geometry

- Some users find it helpful to visualize or draw symbols representing the codes. Sacred geometry, such as mandalas or specific numeric patterns, can act as a focus point during meditation.

Daily Practices with Healing Codes

To incorporate quantum healing codes into daily life, consistency is key. Here are some practical ways to make them a regular part of your routine:

Morning Activation: Begin your day by meditating with the Code of Harmony (432 Hz) to set a tone of balance and positivity.

Stress Management: During moments of stress or anxiety, activate the Code of Emotional Release (396 Hz) to ground yourself and let go of negative emotions.

Physical Recovery: Use the Code of Vitality (285 Hz) after exercise or when recovering from physical strain to promote cellular repair.

Evening Reflection: Before bed, activate the Code of Divine Connection (852 Hz) to clear your mind and deepen your spiritual awareness.

By weaving these codes into your daily practices, you create a consistent energetic environment that supports healing and growth.

Real-Life Applications of Healing Codes

The versatility of core healing codes makes them applicable in various scenarios. Here are a few examples:

Health Challenges: Those experiencing chronic pain or illness can use the Code of Vitality to support traditional treatments.

Emotional Healing: Individuals working through grief or trauma may find solace in the Code of Emotional Release.

Spiritual Growth: Seekers on a journey of self-discovery can use the Code of Divine Connection to deepen their practice.

Many practitioners report profound transformations, such as reduced stress, improved health, and a greater sense of purpose, by consistently using healing codes.

Enhancing the Codes' Power

For those seeking to deepen their connection with the codes, consider these advanced techniques:

Crystal Amplification

 - Pair healing codes with crystals that resonate with similar frequencies. For instance, use rose quartz with the Code of Love (528 Hz) or amethyst with the Code of Divine Connection (852 Hz).

Water Programming

 - Infuse water with the intention of a healing code by meditating with it and visualizing the code's frequency entering the water. Drinking this programmed water enhances the code's effect.

Energy Circuits

- Create an energetic circuit by placing your hands over your heart or solar plexus while meditating on a code. This helps direct the energy where it is most needed.

The Limitless Potential of Healing Codes

The core healing codes represent just the beginning of quantum healing possibilities. These foundational codes can be customized and combined to address unique challenges, creating a personalized roadmap to health and harmony.

By mastering these codes, you unlock the potential to not only heal yourself but also contribute to the healing of others and the collective energy field.

Quantum Healing Codes invite you to become an active participant in your own healing journey. With practice, intention, and openness, these codes can transform every aspect of your life, revealing the limitless power within.

Coming up...

In the next chapter, we'll explore how sound and light can further amplify the power of healing codes, deepening their impact and accelerating the process of transformation.

Prepare to step into a realm where vibration and frequency become the language of healing.

ECNAL VER

CH 5 Activating the Codes Through Sound and Light

The activation of quantum healing codes is an intricate yet accessible process that combines the universal language of sound and light to unlock their transformative potential. These codes are not merely abstract concepts but are energetic frequencies that can be accessed and amplified through tools available to everyone.

In this chapter, we will explore how sound and light can serve as powerful conduits for activating quantum healing codes, bringing harmony and balance to the physical, emotional, and spiritual dimensions of life.

The Connection Between Frequencies and Healing

At the heart of quantum healing codes lies the principle that everything in the universe vibrates at specific frequencies. Both sound and light are manifestations of vibrational energy, and they have the ability to resonate with and influence the energetic patterns of the human body.

By aligning these vibrations with specific quantum healing codes, we can stimulate healing processes at the cellular level and beyond.

Sound waves penetrate deeply into the body, affecting not only physical structures but also the emotional and energetic fields. Similarly, light, with its electromagnetic properties, interacts with the body's biofield to trigger biochemical and energetic responses.

Together, sound and light create a synergistic effect, amplifying the power of quantum healing codes and enhancing their impact.

The Role of Sound in Activating Healing Codes

Sound has been used for millennia as a tool for healing, from ancient chants and mantras to modern sound therapy techniques. In the context of quantum healing codes, sound acts as a carrier wave, delivering the specific vibrational frequencies of the codes to the body and energy field.

Solfeggio Frequencies and Quantum Codes

The solfeggio frequencies, a set of six specific tones, are particularly effective in activating healing codes. Each tone resonates with a specific aspect of the body or psyche:

396 Hz: Liberates guilt and fear, aligning with emotional healing codes.

528 Hz: Facilitates DNA repair and transformation, resonating with physical healing codes.

741 Hz: Promotes detoxification and problem-solving, aligning with mental clarity codes.

These frequencies can be integrated with quantum healing codes by listening to them during meditation or reciting the codes aloud while the frequencies play in the background.

Mantras and Vocalizations

The human voice is one of the most powerful tools for activating healing codes. When a code is vocalized with intention, it resonates not only within the speaker's body but also with the surrounding energetic field.

Repeating a healing code as a mantra, either silently or aloud, can deepen its impact.

Tuning Forks and Instruments

Instruments such as tuning forks, crystal bowls, and gongs can be used to generate pure, resonant frequencies that align with quantum codes.

For example, a tuning fork tuned to 528 Hz can amplify a code designed for cellular repair, creating a harmonious environment for healing.

The Role of Light in Activating Healing Codes

Light, like sound, carries energy that can be harnessed to activate quantum healing codes. Different wavelengths of light correspond to various frequencies, making light therapy a versatile and effective method.

Color Therapy and Chakra Alignment

Each color in the visible spectrum corresponds to a specific frequency and energy center (chakra) in the body:

  Red: Vitality and grounding, activating codes for physical strength.

Green: Balance and healing, aligning with heart-centered codes.

Violet: Intuition and spiritual growth, resonating with higher consciousness codes.

By visualizing or exposing oneself to a specific color while focusing on a quantum healing code, the energy of the code is magnified.

Biophoton Emission and Healing Codes

The body naturally emits biophotons—tiny particles of light that carry information. Quantum healing codes can interact with these biophotons, creating a feedback loop that enhances cellular communication and healing.

Techniques such as photobiomodulation, which uses low-level lasers or LED lights, can amplify this interaction.

Visualization and Light Meditation

Visualization is a powerful method for using light to activate healing codes. Imagine the code as a radiant, luminous symbol, shining in a specific color that resonates with its purpose.

As you focus on this image, see the light permeating your body and energy field, spreading the healing vibration of the code.

Techniques for Combining Sound and Light

The true power of quantum healing codes emerges when sound and light are used together. The integration of these elements creates a multidimensional healing experience that reaches deep into the quantum fabric of existence.

Creating a Healing Ritual

- Choose a healing code that aligns with your current needs.
- Select a corresponding solfeggio frequency or sound therapy tool.
- Visualize the code as a glowing symbol surrounded by light in a color that resonates with its purpose.
- Play the sound while focusing on the visualization, allowing the vibrations of sound and light to merge and activate the code.

Sound-Light Breathing

This technique combines breathwork with sound and light to amplify healing:

- Sit in a quiet, comfortable space.
- Inhale deeply, imagining light in a specific color entering your body.
- Exhale slowly, vocalizing the healing code or its corresponding frequency (e.g., "528").
- Repeat this process for several minutes, allowing the sound and light to work together.

Using Technology for Activation

Modern tools such as sound healing apps and light therapy devices can assist in activating quantum healing codes. For example, an app that plays solfeggio tones can be paired with a colored LED lamp to create a synchronized sound-light environment.

Practical Applications of Sound and Light Activation

The activation of quantum healing codes through sound and light can be applied in various contexts:

Personal Healing

Individuals can use these techniques for self-care, addressing issues such as stress, pain, and emotional imbalances.

Group Healing

In a group setting, sound and light can create a collective resonance that enhances the healing experience for everyone involved. Group meditations or sound baths are excellent opportunities to work with quantum codes.

Professional Practice

Practitioners in fields such as energy healing, massage therapy, or counseling can incorporate sound and light activation into their sessions, providing a holistic approach to client care.

Case Study: Transformative Results

To illustrate the power of sound and light in activating quantum healing codes, consider the case of Sarah, a woman struggling with chronic anxiety.

By focusing on a healing code for emotional resilience, visualizing it in soothing green light, and pairing it with the 396 Hz solfeggio frequency, Sarah experienced profound shifts.

Over a period of weeks, her anxiety lessened, her sleep improved, and she felt more balanced and empowered.

Integrating Sound and Light Activation into Daily Life

The beauty of activating quantum healing codes through sound and light is that it can be seamlessly integrated into daily routines:

- Start your morning with a sound-light meditation to set the tone for the day.
- Use these techniques during breaks to reset and recharge.
- End your day with a focused healing session to release stress and promote restful sleep.

Unlock Healing

The activation of quantum healing codes through sound and light is a transformative practice that taps into the deepest layers of our being. By aligning with the vibrational essence of these universal tools, we can unlock profound healing potential and live in greater harmony with ourselves and the world.

Whether you are addressing physical ailments, emotional wounds, or spiritual growth, sound and light provide the keys to activating the codes that can lead to wholeness and vitality.

ECNAL VER

CH 6 Emotional Healing Codes

Emotional healing is at the core of human transformation. Our emotions serve as powerful drivers of health, well-being, and behavior.

When left unresolved, negative emotions can manifest as physical ailments, mental health challenges, and spiritual blockages. In this chapter, we explore the role of **Quantum Healing Codes** in addressing and transforming emotional wounds, creating a pathway to greater inner peace and vitality.

The Connection Between Emotions and Energy

Emotions are not just fleeting feelings; they are energetic frequencies that affect our body and mind. Each emotion carries a specific vibration—love resonates at a high frequency, while fear and anger operate at lower vibrations.

When negative emotions dominate our energetic field, they disrupt the natural flow of energy, leading to blockages.

Quantum Healing Codes act as energetic keys to unlock these blockages. By introducing specific vibrational patterns, these codes realign the emotional frequencies, helping to restore balance and harmony. They enable us to release trapped emotions, heal past traumas, and build resilience for future challenges.

Key Emotional Healing Codes

Quantum Healing Codes for emotional well-being are designed to address specific needs, from alleviating stress and anxiety to fostering forgiveness and self-love. Below are some foundational codes and their functions:

Code for Releasing Fear

Fear is one of the most *paralyzing* emotions, often preventing growth and self-expression. The **Code for Releasing Fear** operates at a frequency that dissolves the energetic hold fear has on the body and mind.

Activation: Visualize a glowing light entering your heart center, carrying the intention to dissolve fear. Chant or hum the sound associated with this code, such as a calming "Ohm."

Code for Letting Go of Grief

Grief can linger in the heart and create stagnation. The **Code for Letting Go of Grief** helps release this heavy energy, making space for acceptance and healing.

Activation: Meditate on the symbol of a flowing river, visualizing your grief being carried away. Use the corresponding sound frequency, like 396 Hz, to aid in emotional release.

Code for Forgiveness

Forgiveness, whether of oneself or others, is essential for emotional liberation. The **Code for Forgiveness** shifts the energetic field, allowing compassion and understanding to replace resentment.

Activation: Focus on the image of a bridge connecting you and the person or situation you need to forgive. Repeat the affirmation: "I release this for my peace."

Code for Enhancing Self-Love

Self-love is the foundation of all emotional healing. This code strengthens your connection to your true self, reminding you of your inherent worth.

Activation: Place your hand over your heart and visualize a golden light expanding outward. Breathe deeply and repeat, "I am enough. I am love."

How to Use Emotional Healing Codes

The effectiveness of Quantum Healing Codes lies in their proper activation and consistent practice. Here are some steps to integrate these codes into your emotional healing journey:

Identify the Emotional Blockage

Begin by identifying the emotions that need attention. Are you holding onto anger, sadness, or guilt? Acknowledge these feelings without judgment, as awareness is the first step to healing.

Select the Appropriate Code

Choose the Quantum Healing Code that aligns with the emotional challenge you're addressing. You may use one code at a time or combine codes for a more comprehensive healing session.

Prepare Your Space

Create a quiet, distraction-free environment. Dim the lights, light a candle, or play soothing music to enhance the healing atmosphere.

Activate the Code

Use the specific activation method for your chosen code, which might include visualization, sound, or affirmations.

For instance, humming or chanting the associated sound frequency helps you resonate with the code's vibration.

Focus and Release

As you work with the code, focus on releasing the targeted emotion. Imagine the negative energy dissipating from your body, being replaced with light and calm.

Close with Gratitude

End the session by expressing gratitude for the healing process. This reinforces the energetic shift and helps anchor the new emotional state.

The Science of Emotional Healing Codes

Quantum Healing Codes are not merely abstract concepts; they are supported by scientific principles of energy and vibration. Research in neuroscience and epigenetics shows that emotions have a tangible effect on our physical health.

Chronic stress, for example, triggers inflammation, while positive emotions like gratitude and love promote healing and regeneration.

Quantum Healing Codes leverage the science of resonance and entrainment. When the body is exposed to a specific frequency, it naturally begins to align with it—a process known as entrainment.

By introducing high-frequency codes into the body's energy field, these codes help recalibrate emotions, bringing them into a state of coherence.

Real-Life Applications of Emotional Healing Codes

Many individuals have experienced profound transformations using Quantum Healing Codes. Below are a few examples of how these codes have been applied in real-world scenarios:

Case Study: Overcoming Anxiety

Lisa, a 35-year-old teacher, struggled with chronic anxiety. Using the **Code for Releasing Fear**, she dedicated 15 minutes each day to meditation and sound activation. Within a month, she reported feeling calmer and more in control of her thoughts.

Case Study: Healing from Heartbreak

After a painful breakup, David used the **Code for Letting Go of Grief**. He visualized his emotions flowing out like water and listened to the sound frequency of **396 Hz**. Over time, he felt a renewed sense of hope and openness to new relationships.

Case Study: Cultivating Self-Worth

Maria, who struggled with self-esteem issues, embraced the **Code for Enhancing Self-Love**. By combining affirmations and visualization, she transformed her inner dialogue, leading to improved confidence and self-acceptance.

Combining Emotional Healing Codes with Other Practices

Quantum Healing Codes are versatile and can be integrated with other healing modalities for enhanced results:

Meditation and Breathwork

Incorporate codes into your meditation or breathwork routine for deeper emotional release and grounding.

Journaling

Write about the emotions you're working to heal. Pair this reflective practice with the activation of healing codes to solidify the process.

Reiki and Energy Healing

Use **Quantum Healing Codes** alongside energy healing techniques like Reiki to amplify their effects.

Benefits of Emotional Healing with Quantum Codes

The benefits of using Quantum Healing Codes for emotional healing extend beyond immediate relief. They include:

Improved Relationships: Releasing resentment and cultivating forgiveness fosters healthier connections.

Increased Resilience: Addressing unresolved emotions equips you to handle future challenges with grace.

Enhanced Physical Health: Emotional healing reduces stress and promotes overall well-being.

Spiritual Growth: Letting go of emotional baggage clears the path for deeper spiritual awareness and alignment.

Challenges and How to Overcome Them

While **Quantum Healing Codes** are powerful, the process may not always be straightforward. Here are common challenges and ways to address them:

Resistance to Change

Some individuals may feel resistant to letting go of familiar emotional patterns. Counter this by setting clear intentions and practicing patience.

Emotional Overwhelm

Working through deep-seated emotions can feel intense. Take breaks as needed and focus on grounding exercises to stay balanced.

Doubt in the Process

Doubt can hinder the effectiveness of healing codes. Build trust in the process by starting with small, manageable goals and observing incremental progress.

Final Thoughts on Emotional Healing Codes

Emotional healing is an essential step on the path to holistic well-being, and Quantum Healing Codes offer a transformative tool for this journey.

By aligning your emotional frequencies with these powerful codes, you can release the weight of past pain, open your heart to love and joy, and step into a life of balance and harmony.

Trust the process, practice consistently, and allow the codes to guide you toward the emotional liberation you deserve.

CH 7 Physical Healing Codes

The human body is an intricate tapestry of energy, frequency, and vibration. At its most fundamental level, it is composed of atoms and subatomic particles that vibrate at specific frequencies.

Quantum Healing Codes, as a set of frequencies and energetic patterns, can communicate directly with the body's energetic field to promote physical healing.

This chapter explores the use of physical healing codes, their mechanisms, and practical techniques to activate them for cellular regeneration, pain relief, and overall physical vitality.

The Quantum Basis of Physical Healing Codes

The concept of Quantum Healing Codes for physical health stems from the idea that every organ, tissue, and cell in the body resonates at its own unique frequency.

When these frequencies are disrupted—whether by trauma, illness, or emotional stress—the body falls out of balance, leading to disease or discomfort. Physical healing codes act as a corrective mechanism, helping to realign these frequencies and restore harmony.

Scientific research supports the idea that frequencies and vibrations can impact physical matter. For example, studies in cymatics—the study of how sound affects matter—demonstrate how specific frequencies create geometric patterns in materials like water or sand.

Similarly, the human body, composed largely of water, is highly responsive to external frequencies, making it a suitable medium for healing through Quantum Healing Codes.

Understanding Physical Healing Codes

Physical healing codes are designed to address the energetic imbalances that underlie physical ailments. These codes can be used for:

Cellular regeneration: Promoting the repair and renewal of damaged cells.

Pain relief: Alleviating chronic pain by targeting its energetic root causes.

Immune support: Enhancing the body's natural defense mechanisms.

Inflammation reduction: Calming overactive inflammatory responses in the body.

Each code corresponds to a specific intention or outcome, which is then expressed as a unique combination of frequencies, visualizations, or symbols.

For example, a code for pain relief might involve focusing on a sequence of numbers, colors, or sound vibrations that interact with the body's energy field to neutralize discomfort.

How Physical Healing Codes Work

Physical healing codes operate through the principle of resonance. When a healing code is introduced into the body's energetic field, it resonates with the affected area, gently encouraging it to return to its natural frequency.

This process can be compared to tuning a musical instrument: just as a tuning fork can bring a piano string back into harmony, Quantum Healing Codes can realign the frequencies of the body.

The process of activating physical healing codes typically involves the following steps:

Intention: Setting a clear and focused intention is the foundation of any healing work. The user must define their desired outcome, such as alleviating joint pain or accelerating recovery from an injury.

Visualization or Symbol Activation: Many physical healing codes are represented as geometric patterns, symbols, or sequences of numbers. Visualizing these symbols or writing them down activates their energetic potential.

Frequency Engagement: Sound, light, or meditation can amplify the healing process. Playing specific sound frequencies (e.g., solfeggio tones) or exposing the body to particular colors enhances the impact of the codes.

Repetition: Healing codes often require consistent application to fully integrate with the body's energy. Repeating the code multiple times daily can create lasting effects.

Using Healing Codes for Specific Physical Ailments

Here are examples of how physical healing codes can be applied to address common health concerns:

Cellular Regeneration

Physical healing codes can be used to stimulate cellular repair and renewal. For example, after an injury, the body focuses energy on repairing damaged tissue. A healing code designed for cellular regeneration might involve visualizing the damaged area surrounded by a glowing golden light while repeating the numerical sequence **528-111**, known for promoting DNA repair. Pairing this visualization with deep breathing and listening to solfeggio frequencies enhances the healing process.

Pain Relief

Pain is often an indication of energetic blockages or imbalances. A physical healing code for pain relief could involve visualizing a swirling vortex of energy drawing pain away from the affected area. The numerical sequence **417-639** might be used, as these frequencies are associated with clearing negativity and fostering harmony. Chanting or humming these frequencies adds a vibrational layer that interacts with the body's energy field.

Immune System Support

A strong immune system is essential for physical health. Healing codes for immune support might include sequences like **741-852**, which are believed to detoxify the body and strengthen resilience. Visualizing the immune system as a shield of radiant white light while meditating on these numbers can amplify their effects.

Reducing Inflammation

Chronic inflammation can lead to numerous health issues, from arthritis to heart disease. Healing codes targeting inflammation often involve calming colors, such as blue or green, which promote relaxation and balance. The sequence **396-528** can be used in conjunction with cooling visualizations, such as imagining a soothing waterfall washing over the inflamed area.

Techniques for Activating Physical Healing Codes

Visualization

Visualization is one of the most accessible ways to activate healing codes. By focusing on specific images, shapes, or colors associated with the code, you can direct energy to the targeted area.

For example, imagining a glowing orb of energy radiating from your hands to a sore muscle can facilitate healing.

Sound Healing

Sound plays a critical role in activating physical healing codes. Using tuning forks, singing bowls, or digital recordings of specific frequencies can help attune the body's energy field to the desired code.

Pairing sound healing with breathwork enhances its impact.

Writing and Drawing

Physically writing or drawing the healing code on paper—or even directly on the skin using non-toxic ink—can create a tangible connection to its energy.

Some practitioners write codes on adhesive bandages and place them over the affected area.

Light Therapy

Exposing the body to colored light that corresponds to the healing code's frequency can be highly effective. For example, green light is often used for inflammation, while red light supports circulation and vitality.

Meditation and Affirmation

Meditative focus combined with affirmations strengthens the intention behind the healing code. A simple affirmation like "My body is healing and whole" can be repeated while focusing on the code.

Real-Life Applications of Physical Healing Codes

The power of physical healing codes lies in their ability to address a wide range of conditions. Here are some real-life applications:

Post-Surgical Recovery: A patient recovering from surgery can use healing codes to accelerate tissue repair and minimize pain. Visualizing golden light while focusing on the sequence **528-639** can assist in recovery.

Chronic Illness Management: Individuals with chronic illnesses, such as fibromyalgia or migraines, have reported significant relief by integrating healing codes into their daily routines.

Athletic Performance and Recovery: Athletes can use healing codes to improve performance and recover more quickly from injuries. A sequence like **852-963** can be used to promote mental clarity and physical endurance.

When to Use Healing Codes

Physical healing codes can be used proactively as well as reactively. Incorporating them into daily wellness practices can help maintain balance and prevent illness.

For example, meditating with a general healing code like **528-852** once a day can enhance overall vitality. In times of acute illness or injury, more focused and frequent use of the codes may be necessary.

Tap Into the Potential

The body's capacity for self-healing is profound, and Quantum Healing Codes provide a tool to tap into this potential. By harmonizing the body's frequencies, these codes can support physical health and vitality in ways that are both profound and transformative.

In the quantum field, healing is not a matter of chance—it is a matter of resonance, intention, and alignment. Through the regular use of physical healing codes, anyone can unlock their innate ability to restore balance and thrive.

ECNAL VER

CH 8 Spiritual Awakening Codes

Unlocking Higher Consciousness and Connecting with Universal Energy

In the intricate tapestry of quantum healing, spiritual awakening codes stand as the bridge between the physical, emotional, and spiritual dimensions of our existence.

These codes are designed to elevate our consciousness, align us with the universe's higher frequencies, and open gateways to profound spiritual growth.

By accessing and activating these spiritual awakening codes, individuals can experience a deep connection with their inner selves and the universal energy that governs all existence.

The Purpose of Spiritual Awakening Codes

At their core, spiritual awakening codes are quantum frequencies encoded with the essence of universal truths. These codes act as keys to unlock the latent potential within each individual, allowing for the awakening of higher states of awareness and connection.

They enable individuals to transcend the limitations of the physical realm and tap into the infinite energy field of the quantum universe.

These codes work by harmonizing the vibrations of the mind, body, and spirit, facilitating a state of coherence that aligns the individual with the flow of universal energy.

This alignment often manifests as heightened intuition, a sense of inner peace, and an expanded perspective on life.

How Spiritual Awakening Codes Work

Quantum healing codes function by resonating with the vibrational frequencies of the body's energy centers, also known as chakras.

Spiritual awakening codes specifically target the higher chakras, such as the third eye (Ajna) and crown (Sahasrara), which are associated with intuition, insight, and connection to the divine.

Activation of the Third Eye Chakra:

The third eye chakra is the center of intuition and inner vision. When activated using spiritual codes, individuals often experience clarity in their thoughts and a deeper understanding of their purpose. The code for this activation resonates at a frequency designed to stimulate insight and dissolve mental blocks.

Opening the Crown Chakra:

The crown chakra connects us to universal energy and divine consciousness. Spiritual awakening codes aligned with this chakra promote a sense of unity with the cosmos and foster a profound sense of spiritual enlightenment.

Synchronizing the Heart Chakra:

While the heart chakra primarily governs emotions, its role in spiritual awakening is significant. Codes that activate the heart chakra enable individuals to connect with others on a soul level, fostering compassion and unconditional love.

Key Spiritual Awakening Codes and Their Frequencies

Below are some of the primary codes used in spiritual awakening, along with their corresponding intentions:

Code 777 – Unity and Oneness:

This code symbolizes the divine connection and unity with universal consciousness. It resonates with frequencies of harmony and integration, helping individuals feel at one with the cosmos.

Code 963 Hz – The Frequency of Light:

Often referred to as the "God frequency," **963 Hz** activates the pineal gland and promotes spiritual enlightenment. It enhances one's connection to the divine and aids in the experience of cosmic consciousness.

Code 888 – Abundance and Spiritual Alignment:

This code harmonizes with the energy of spiritual abundance, aligning the individual's desires with the universe's provision.

It is a powerful tool for manifesting spiritual growth and blessings.

432 Hz – Universal Harmony:

This frequency aligns with the vibration of nature and the universe. It is often used to bring balance and serenity, allowing the individual to feel deeply connected to the natural order.

Methods for Activating Spiritual Awakening Codes

To fully harness the potential of these codes, individuals must consciously integrate them into their spiritual practices. Below are several methods to activate and benefit from these codes:

Meditative Visualization:

- Begin by finding a quiet and comfortable space to meditate.
- Visualize the code as a glowing symbol or sequence of numbers, vibrating with energy.
- Focus on the code's meaning and its connection to your desired spiritual outcome.
- Allow the energy of the code to infuse your entire being, visualizing it harmonizing with your chakras.

Chanting and Sound Therapy:

Chanting the code, either as a number sequence or a sound frequency, can activate its vibration within the body.

For example, chant "**777**" slowly and rhythmically while focusing on the feeling of unity.

Alternatively, use sound therapy tools like tuning forks or singing bowls tuned to specific frequencies like **963 Hz** or **432 Hz**.

Sacred Geometry:

Many spiritual awakening codes are linked to sacred geometric patterns.

Draw or visualize these patterns while meditating on the corresponding code.

Sacred geometry helps the mind focus on the universal truths embedded in the code.

Affirmation and Intention Setting:

Pair the code with affirmations that align with its purpose. For instance:

For **Code 963 Hz**: "I am one with the divine light and infinite wisdom."

For **Code 777**: "I embrace my connection to the universe and all its energy."

Speak these affirmations aloud or write them down while focusing on the code.

Journaling and Reflection:

Write the code in a journal and reflect on its significance in your life.

Combine this practice with gratitude journaling to amplify its effects.

The Role of Intuition in Working with Spiritual Codes

Spiritual awakening codes are not rigid tools; they are fluid and adaptable, responding to the intentions and needs of the user. Intuition plays a vital role in their activation.

As you work with these codes, trust your instincts to guide you toward the methods and practices that resonate most deeply.

For example, you may feel drawn to a particular frequency or code even if it doesn't correspond to your initial intention. This is a sign that your energy field is aligning with that code for a specific purpose, often one that your conscious mind may not yet recognize.

Practical Applications of Spiritual Awakening Codes

Daily Spiritual Practice:

Integrate these codes into your morning or evening routine to set the tone for the day or promote relaxation and reflection.

Healing Emotional Blocks:

Use spiritual awakening codes to address and heal deep-seated emotional wounds that may be hindering your spiritual growth.

Enhancing Relationships:

Codes such as **432 Hz** can be used to promote harmony and understanding in personal relationships, fostering deeper connections.

Manifesting Spiritual Goals:

Whether you seek greater intuition, alignment with your purpose, or a sense of peace, spiritual codes can help manifest these aspirations.

Real-Life Transformations Through Spiritual Awakening Codes

Many individuals who have worked with spiritual awakening codes report profound changes in their lives.

They speak of feeling more connected to their inner selves and the world around them, experiencing a sense of clarity, and finding renewed purpose in their spiritual journeys.

One individual shared their experience of using **Code 963 Hz** during meditation. Within weeks, they noticed a heightened sense of intuition and began receiving insights that helped them navigate personal challenges with grace and confidence.

Another practitioner who worked with **Code 777** described feeling a deep sense of unity with the people and environments they encountered. This newfound connection transformed their relationships and allowed them to approach life with a more open heart.

Challenges and Overcoming Resistance

As with any spiritual practice, some individuals may face resistance or skepticism when working with spiritual awakening codes.

These challenges often stem from mental blocks or doubts about the efficacy of the codes. To overcome this, approach the practice with an open mind and a willingness to explore.

Trust in the process and allow the codes to work at their own pace.

Embracing the Journey of Awakening

Spiritual awakening codes are a powerful tool for those seeking to expand their consciousness and connect with the universal energy that permeates all existence.

By integrating these codes into your life, you open the door to profound transformation and a deeper understanding of your place in the cosmos. As you embark on this journey, remember that the path to spiritual awakening is as much about the process as it is about the destination.

Trust in the codes, trust in yourself, and trust in the infinite possibilities of the quantum universe.

CH 9 Creating Your Personal Quantum Healing Code

The concept of **Quantum Healing Codes** unlocks a universe of personalized potential. These codes, rooted in the quantum fabric of the universe, offer unique pathways to physical, emotional, and spiritual healing.

In this chapter, we delve into the process of crafting your **personal quantum healing code**—an energetic tool tailored to your specific needs and aspirations. By combining intention, frequency, and symbolic resonance, you can design a code that harmonizes with your unique energetic blueprint.

Why Create a Personal Quantum Healing Code?

Healing is a deeply personal journey. While universal codes are powerful and effective, a code created specifically for you has the potential to resonate more profoundly with your energy field. Personalized healing codes:

- Address your specific physical, emotional, or spiritual challenges.
- Amplify your connection to the quantum field by aligning with your intentions.
- Empower you to take an active role in your healing process.

Creating your personal quantum code is not just about healing—it's a journey of self-discovery and alignment with the greater universal energy.

Step 1: Clarify Your Intention

The first step in crafting your personal quantum healing code is to clarify your intention. The universe responds to clarity, and the more specific your intention, the more powerful your code will be. To define your intention:

Identify Your Need: Reflect on the area of your life that requires healing or growth. Is it physical pain, emotional trauma, or spiritual stagnation?

Phrase It Clearly: Write your intention as a positive, present-tense statement. For example, instead of saying, "I want to stop feeling anxious," reframe it as "I am calm, peaceful, and grounded."

Focus on Emotion: Anchor your intention with an emotional state. How do you want to feel when the code activates?

Take time to meditate or journal to ensure your intention feels authentic and aligned with your higher self.

Step 2: Choose Symbols and Elements

Symbols are powerful carriers of meaning and energy. In quantum healing, they act as conduits for intention, helping you communicate with the quantum field. To create your personal code, select symbols and elements that resonate with you:

Sacred Geometry: Shapes like circles, triangles, and spirals are universally recognized in quantum and spiritual realms. Each shape carries a unique vibrational frequency.

Numbers: Numerology can provide insights into the energetic significance of numbers. For example, 1 represents unity, 3 symbolizes creativity, and 8 signifies abundance.

Colors: Each color has a specific vibration. Blue can evoke calmness, green represents healing, and gold symbolizes divine connection.

Personal Symbols: Incorporate symbols that hold personal significance, such as a family heirloom, a meaningful location, or an image from a dream.

Experiment with combining these elements until the code begins to "feel" right to you.

Step 3: Integrate Frequencies

Quantum healing codes are vibrational in nature, meaning they interact with your energetic field at a frequency level. To enhance your code, you can integrate specific sound or light frequencies:

Solfeggio Frequencies: These ancient sound frequencies are known for their healing properties. For example, 528 Hz is associated with DNA repair, while 741 Hz helps detoxify the body.

Chakra Frequencies: Align your code with the frequency of the chakra related to your intention. For example, use 396 Hz for root chakra grounding or 852 Hz for third-eye intuition.

Personal Frequencies: Experiment with sounds or tones that resonate deeply with you, such as a favorite piece of music or the vibration of a singing bowl.

You can include these frequencies as part of your meditation practice when activating your code.

Step 4: Design and Visualize Your Code

Once you have chosen your symbols and frequencies, it's time to design your quantum healing code. This is where creativity meets intuition:

- Draw the Code: Use pen and paper or digital tools to sketch your code. Combine your chosen symbols into a harmonious design that feels intuitively correct.
- Add Layers of Meaning: Include numbers, colors, and patterns that correspond to your intention.
- Visualize the Code in Action: Close your eyes and imagine your code activating. Picture its energy radiating outward, healing and balancing your body, mind, and spirit.

Your code does not have to be artistically perfect—it simply needs to feel aligned with your energy.

Step 5: Activate Your Code

A healing code is only as effective as the intention and energy you invest in it. Activation is the process of imbuing the code with power. Here's how to activate your personal quantum healing code:

Meditate: Sit in a quiet space and focus on your breath. Bring your mind to a calm, centered state.

Set Your Intention: Hold your code in your hands or visualize it in your mind. Speak your intention out loud or silently, affirming the purpose of the code.

Charge the Code: Use a crystal, candle, or other energetic tool to charge your code. For example, place a quartz crystal over your code or hold it in sunlight.

Visualize Activation: Imagine your code coming to life, glowing with energy, and harmonizing with your body's frequency.

Repeat this activation process as often as needed to reinforce the code's power.

Step 6: Use and Maintain Your Code

Once activated, your code becomes a living tool for healing and growth. Incorporate it into your daily routine:

Meditate with the Code: Use your code as a focal point during meditation to strengthen its effects.

Display the Code: Place the code in a visible location, such as your workspace, bedroom, or altar.

Combine with Healing Practices: Use the code alongside other practices like yoga, sound healing, or breathwork.

Revisit and Update: As your needs and intentions evolve, feel free to refine or redesign your code.

Treat your code as a dynamic part of your healing journey, capable of growing and adapting with you.

Real-Life Applications of Personal Quantum Healing Codes

Creating and using a personal quantum healing code can lead to profound transformations. Here are a few examples of how personalized codes have impacted others:

Physical Healing: A woman with chronic migraines created a code featuring the spiral (symbolizing release) and the number 8 (infinity and balance). By meditating with the code daily, she reported significant relief from her pain within weeks.

Emotional Recovery: After a traumatic breakup, a man designed a code incorporating the color green (heart chakra healing) and the number 7 (spiritual growth). The code helped him process his emotions and move forward with newfound peace.

Spiritual Alignment: A seeker created a code to deepen their intuition and connection to the divine. Using sacred geometry and solfeggio frequencies, they experienced heightened clarity and synchronicity in their life.

These examples highlight the versatility and power of personalized quantum healing codes.

The Journey of Self-Empowerment

Creating your personal quantum healing code is more than a healing tool—it's an act of empowerment. It teaches you to listen to your inner wisdom, trust your intuition, and take charge of your well-being.

Each step in this process brings you closer to your authentic self and strengthens your connection to the quantum field.

By crafting and activating your unique code, you become an active participant in your healing journey, unlocking limitless potential for transformation and growth.

In the next chapter, we will explore how to use quantum healing codes to help others, sharing insights and techniques for applying these powerful tools in group settings or distant healing practices.

CH 10 Healing Others with Quantum Codes

Quantum healing codes hold immense potential not just for personal transformation but also for healing others. The universal principles governing these codes make them adaptable for various applications, allowing practitioners to extend their use beyond self-healing.

This chapter explores the methods, ethical considerations, and techniques for using quantum healing codes to assist others in their journey toward wellness and balance.

The Power of Shared Energetic Frequencies

Healing others with quantum healing codes is grounded in the principle of shared energetic frequencies. At the quantum level, we are all connected through an intricate web of energy fields.

This interconnectedness allows healing frequencies to flow from one individual to another, whether in person or at a distance.

The quantum field, often referred to as the universal matrix or the divine grid, acts as a bridge. When you activate a quantum healing code with intention and focus, the vibrations resonate through this field, aligning the recipient's energy with the healing frequency encoded in the quantum structure.

This process is not limited by space or time, making distant healing just as effective as direct interaction.

Preparing to Heal Others

Establishing Intentions

Before using quantum healing codes to help someone else, it's crucial to set clear intentions. Healing is most effective when it is aligned with the recipient's highest good and free from personal expectations. Ask yourself:

- What is the purpose of this healing session?
- Am I respecting the autonomy and readiness of the recipient?
- How can I ensure this healing process is unconditional?

Intentions act as the guiding force for quantum codes, ensuring that the energy flows precisely where it is needed.

Creating a Sacred Space

Healing requires an environment conducive to energy flow. Whether you're working in person or remotely, create a sacred space that fosters focus and tranquility.

This space doesn't have to be elaborate but should be free from distractions. Use elements like soft lighting, soothing sounds, and calming aromas to elevate the energy of the space.

Centering Yourself

Before initiating the healing process, take a few moments to center yourself. This can be achieved through deep breathing, meditation, or grounding exercises. A centered state ensures that your energy field remains balanced, allowing you to channel the quantum codes effectively.

Techniques for Healing Others

Direct Healing

In direct healing, you interact with the recipient face-to-face, using quantum healing codes to address their needs. The process typically involves the following steps:

Energy Scanning: Begin by scanning the recipient's energy field. This can be done intuitively or with tools like a pendulum. Identify areas of imbalance or stagnation.

Code Activation: Select the quantum healing code that aligns with the recipient's specific needs. For example, a code for cellular regeneration can be used for physical healing, while a code for emotional release may be appropriate for trauma.

Application: Use visualization, touch, or sound to transmit the healing code. For instance, you can visualize the code as a vibrant symbol entering the recipient's energy field, or chant the code's frequency to enhance its vibration.

Integration: Allow the recipient's body and mind to integrate the energy. Encourage them to rest and reflect after the session.

Distant Healing

Quantum codes transcend physical boundaries, making distant healing a powerful option. Here's how to perform distant healing:

Connection: Establish a mental connection with the recipient. This can be done by visualizing their image, speaking their name, or holding an object that represents them.

Code Transmission: Visualize the quantum healing code enveloping the recipient in a field of light. Imagine the vibrations traveling through the quantum field to reach them.

Affirmation: Use affirmations to reinforce the energy transfer. For example, "May this healing energy align with your highest good."

Completion: End the session with gratitude, acknowledging the universal energy that made the healing possible.

Ethical Considerations in Healing Others

When using quantum healing codes to assist others, it is essential to approach the process with integrity and respect. Healing is a deeply personal journey, and practitioners must honor the boundaries and autonomy of the individuals they are helping.

Seek Permission

Always seek permission before initiating a healing session. Even if you feel confident about the benefits of quantum codes, it's important to ensure that the recipient is open and willing to receive the energy.

Unsolicited healing can disrupt their energetic balance and may not align with their personal journey.

Avoid Attachment to Outcomes

As a healer, your role is to facilitate the flow of energy, not to control the results. Avoid becoming attached to specific outcomes, as this can hinder the natural process of healing. Trust that the quantum codes will work in the way that is most beneficial for the recipient.

Respect Confidentiality

Healing sessions often involve sensitive information. Respect the recipient's privacy by keeping their experiences confidential. This builds trust and creates a safe space for them to explore their healing process.

Amplifying Healing with Group Work

Quantum healing codes can also be used in group settings, creating a collective resonance that amplifies the energy. Group healing sessions are particularly effective for addressing shared challenges, such as community grief, global events, or collective trauma.

How to Conduct Group Healing Sessions

Unified Intention: Align the group's intentions before activating the quantum codes. This can be achieved through a shared meditation or prayer.

Code Activation: Introduce the healing codes that resonate with the group's needs. For instance, use codes for unity and harmony when addressing communal challenges.

Collective Visualization: Guide the group in visualizing the quantum codes spreading across the collective energy field, creating waves of healing.

Integration and Reflection: Allow time for participants to integrate the energy and share their experiences.

Tools to Enhance Healing

Several tools and techniques can enhance the effectiveness of quantum healing codes when assisting others:

Crystals: Use crystals to amplify the energy of the codes. For example, clear quartz can enhance clarity, while amethyst supports emotional healing.

Sound Frequencies: Play sound frequencies that correspond to the quantum codes. Instruments like tuning forks, singing bowls, or chimes are particularly effective.

Visualization Guides: Provide the recipient with visual aids, such as images or symbols of the quantum codes, to help them focus on the healing process.

The Role of Intuition in Healing Others

Intuition is a vital aspect of using quantum healing codes. While the codes provide a structured framework, your intuition guides their application.

Pay attention to subtle cues, such as sensations, images, or emotions that arise during the session. These intuitive insights often reveal the deeper needs of the recipient.

Challenges in Healing Others

Healing others with quantum codes can present challenges, particularly if the recipient is resistant or skeptical. In such cases:

- Focus on building trust and explaining the process in simple terms.
- Emphasize that the healing energy works at a subtle level and does not require full belief to be effective.
- Encourage the recipient to remain open to the experience, even if they do not fully understand it.

Healing as a Reciprocal Process

One of the most beautiful aspects of healing others is that it is a reciprocal process. As you channel quantum healing codes for someone else, you also benefit from the high-frequency energy.

This mutual exchange creates a sense of balance and harmony, deepening your connection to the quantum field.

Act of Compassion

Healing others with quantum healing codes is a profound act of compassion and service. By setting intentions, respecting ethical boundaries, and utilizing the techniques outlined in this chapter, you can facilitate transformative healing experiences. Whether working with individuals or groups, the application of quantum codes opens the door to limitless possibilities for health and harmony.

Remember, as you share these codes, you become a conduit for universal energy, fostering healing not only for others but for yourself and the collective consciousness.

CH 11 Troubleshooting and Enhancing Code Effectiveness

The journey of working with quantum healing codes is deeply transformative, but like any path to healing and growth, it may come with challenges.

Understanding and addressing these challenges is essential to unlocking the full potential of the codes.

In this chapter, we explore common obstacles that may arise when using quantum healing codes and provide practical strategies to enhance their effectiveness.

Understanding Resistance to Healing Codes

Resistance to healing codes is often rooted in subconscious patterns or beliefs that conflict with the desired transformation. These patterns can create energetic blocks that impede the codes' ability to harmonize with your energy field.

Resistance may manifest as doubt, fear, or even physical discomfort during activation.

Doubt and Skepticism: Many people approach quantum healing codes with a mix of curiosity and skepticism. While healthy skepticism is natural, excessive doubt can dampen the codes' effects.

Healing codes work best when the user is open to their potential and willing to engage with them fully.

Fear of Change: Deep healing often brings change, which can feel unsettling. The fear of the unknown or losing familiar patterns, even unhealthy ones, can create internal resistance.

Physical or Emotional Discomfort: Sometimes, the body or mind reacts to the codes with temporary discomfort. This reaction is often a sign of energetic release or adjustment, as the codes work to remove old blockages.

Overcoming Resistance

To work through resistance, it is essential to approach the process with patience, self-compassion, and intentional practices that support the codes' integration.

Acknowledgment and Awareness: Recognize and acknowledge the resistance without judgment. Ask yourself: What fears or doubts are surfacing? Simply naming these feelings can diminish their hold on you.

Reaffirm Your Intention: Revisit your reason for using the healing codes. Reaffirming your intention creates a clear energetic focus that aligns your mind, body, and spirit with the codes.

Deep Breathing and Relaxation: Engaging in deep breathing exercises or mindfulness meditation can calm the nervous system and create a receptive state for the codes to work.

Common Challenges and Their Solutions

Lack of Immediate Results

Healing is a process, and while some individuals experience immediate shifts, others may find the effects take time to manifest. This delay can lead to frustration or doubt.

Solution: Trust the process and maintain consistency. Use the codes daily and allow your energy field to adapt to the new frequencies. Journal your experiences to track subtle changes over time.

Difficulty Focusing During Activation

Some people struggle to maintain focus or a clear intention when using the codes, which can dilute their effectiveness.

Solution: Create a dedicated, distraction-free space for your healing work. Use tools like guided meditations, sound frequencies, or visual aids to enhance concentration.

Energetic Overload

Occasionally, users may feel overwhelmed by the intensity of the codes, leading to emotional outbursts or physical fatigue.

Solution: Take a break and allow your system to integrate the changes. Return to the codes at a slower pace or use grounding techniques like walking barefoot or visualizing roots connecting you to the earth.

Energetic Interference

External factors, such as electromagnetic fields (EMFs), toxic environments, or negative relationships, can interfere with the codes' efficacy.

Solution: Minimize exposure to disruptive influences and create a supportive environment. Surround yourself with positive energy, use EMF shields, and practice energetic cleansing techniques, such as smudging or salt baths.

Advanced Techniques to Enhance Effectiveness

As you become more familiar with quantum healing codes, you can explore advanced methods to amplify their power and deepen their integration.

Visualization and Symbolism: Visualization is a powerful tool for aligning with the codes. Picture the healing codes as vibrant, glowing symbols entering your energy field and harmonizing with your being.

Assign personal meaning to each code to strengthen its connection to your intention.

Sound and Frequency Pairing: Pairing the codes with specific sound frequencies, such as solfeggio tones or binaural beats, can enhance their vibrational impact.

Each sound frequency corresponds to a unique healing property, creating a synergy with the codes.

Mantras and Affirmations: Combine the codes with verbal affirmations or mantras that reflect your healing goals. Speaking these affirmations while activating the codes reinforces their energetic imprint.

Sacred Geometry and Visualization Grids: Using sacred geometry patterns as a visual focus while activating the codes can create a more potent energetic alignment. Visualize the codes embedded in these geometric forms, radiating energy throughout your body.

Maintaining Long-Term Effectiveness

Once you've established a consistent practice with quantum healing codes, maintaining their long-term effectiveness requires ongoing attention and care.

Periodic Energy Assessments: Regularly assess your energy field for new imbalances or blockages. This practice helps ensure that you're addressing current needs and adapting your codes accordingly.

Refresh Your Intention: Periodically revisit and refine your intentions to ensure they align with your evolving goals.

Integrate the Codes into Daily Life: Make the codes a natural part of your daily routine by combining them with existing practices, such as yoga, meditation, or journaling.

Connecting with the Quantum Field

The effectiveness of quantum healing codes ultimately depends on your connection to the quantum field—a limitless source of energy and potential. Strengthening this connection enhances your ability to channel the codes' transformative power.

Expand Your Awareness: Engage in practices that expand your awareness of the quantum field, such as meditation, breathwork, or spending time in nature.

Practice Gratitude: Gratitude shifts your energy to a higher frequency, opening the gateway to deeper healing and alignment with the quantum field.

Cultivate Inner Stillness: Inner stillness creates a clear, receptive space for the codes to work. Regularly dedicate time to silence and introspection.

Seeking Support When Needed

It's important to recognize when external support may enhance your healing journey. Seeking guidance from experienced practitioners or mentors can help you navigate challenges and deepen your understanding of the codes.

Healing Circles and Communities: Joining a community of like-minded individuals can provide encouragement and shared wisdom.

Professional Guidance: Work with a healer, therapist, or coach who understands quantum healing codes and can offer personalized support.

Embracing the Learning Process

Working with quantum healing codes is as much about self-discovery as it is about healing. Every challenge you encounter offers an opportunity to grow, refine your practice, and deepen your connection to your inner power.

Remember that healing is a journey, not a destination. The codes are tools that assist in this journey, but the real transformation comes from your willingness to engage with them fully and openly.

As you continue to work with quantum healing codes, you'll find that they not only address specific challenges but also lead you toward a greater understanding of yourself and the infinite possibilities within the quantum field.

With patience, practice, and persistence, you can unlock their full potential and experience profound healing and growth.

CH 12 Living in Harmony with Quantum Codes

Quantum healing codes are not just tools for temporary healing or quick fixes; they are a way of life, a framework for aligning with the energy of the universe. To fully integrate these codes into your daily experience is to embrace a life of balance, vitality, and harmony.

This chapter explores how to live in alignment with quantum healing codes, using them as a guiding principle to sustain long-term physical, emotional, and spiritual health.

Understanding Integration: Beyond the Healing Moment

When working with quantum healing codes, the initial application is often focused on specific issues—physical pain, emotional distress, or spiritual disconnection.

However, the true power of these codes lies in their ability to reshape how we interact with the world around us. By living in harmony with these frequencies, we can create a life where healing is ongoing, resilience is natural, and growth is effortless.

Integration means weaving the codes into the fabric of your life so they become second nature. It's no longer about "using" the codes occasionally but living by their principles consistently.

This requires mindfulness, intention, and a commitment to aligning your thoughts, emotions, and actions with the frequencies of the codes.

Daily Practices to Sustain Harmony

Morning Activation Rituals

Start each day by intentionally activating the quantum healing codes that resonate with your goals. Whether you seek clarity, strength, or peace, set aside a few minutes for visualization or meditation to align with those frequencies. You can visualize the codes, chant their associated sounds, or use light therapy to connect with their energy.

Example: Begin your day with the "Harmony Code" to set a tone of balance. Visualize this code as a glowing symbol in your mind's eye while taking deep, intentional breaths.

Mindful Alignment Throughout the Day

During your daily activities, stay mindful of the quantum frequencies. When you encounter stress, pause and recall the calming energy of specific codes, such as those for patience or courage.

A quick, mental reactivation can instantly shift your state and keep you aligned with your goals.

Example: If you face a difficult conversation, use the "Courage Code." Take a moment to visualize the code or chant its tone before engaging.

Evening Reflection and Recalibration

End your day with a reflective practice. Assess how well you stayed aligned with the quantum healing codes. If there were moments of disconnection or imbalance, use this time to recalibrate by meditating on the "Forgiveness Code" or the "Self-Love Code." This ensures that you enter rest with a clear and balanced energy.

Strengthening Your Connection with the Codes

Journaling with the Codes

Keep a journal to document your experiences with quantum healing codes. Write down the codes you've used, the circumstances in which you applied them, and the outcomes.

Over time, patterns will emerge, helping you understand which codes resonate most with your energy.

Creating a Sacred Space for Healing

Dedicate a physical space in your home for working with the codes. This space can include visual representations of the codes, such as artwork or printed symbols, along with tools like crystals, sound bowls, or light therapy devices.

Entering this space will serve as a signal to your subconscious to align with the quantum frequencies.

Connecting with Nature

Nature is one of the purest expressions of quantum harmony. Spend time in natural settings to deepen your connection with the codes. Whether walking barefoot on the earth or meditating near water, these experiences amplify your ability to align with universal energy.

Using Codes in Relationships

Living in harmony with quantum healing codes can transform how you relate to others. Relationships are energetic exchanges, and when you align your interactions with quantum frequencies, you create a foundation of love, understanding, and mutual respect.

Resolving Conflicts with Healing Codes

Conflict often arises from energetic misalignments. When disagreements occur, introduce the "Compassion Code" or the "Understanding Code" into your energy field. This practice shifts the dynamic, making it easier to find resolutions that benefit everyone involved.

Strengthening Connections

Use codes to deepen bonds with loved ones. For example, activate the "Gratitude Code" when spending time with family or friends to amplify feelings of appreciation and joy.

Setting Energetic Boundaries

In relationships that challenge your peace, the "Protection Code" can help establish healthy boundaries. This code acts as an energetic shield, allowing you to engage without being drained.

Aligning with Purpose and Passion

Quantum healing codes are not limited to personal well-being; they are also tools for achieving higher purpose and passion.

When you live in harmony with these codes, you align with the energy needed to manifest your deepest desires and contribute to the world meaningfully.

Activating the "Purpose Code"

This code helps you gain clarity on your life's mission. Meditate with this code regularly to stay connected with your passions and ensure your actions align with your purpose.

Enhancing Creativity and Flow

Creativity thrives when your energy is aligned. Use the "Inspiration Code" to access creative flow and bring innovative ideas to life. Whether you're an artist, entrepreneur, or problem-solver, this code can help you tap into boundless potential.

Manifesting Abundance

Abundance is a natural byproduct of energetic alignment. The "Abundance Code" works by attuning your frequency to the vibration of prosperity, helping you attract opportunities, resources, and support effortlessly.

Healing the Collective: Quantum Codes for a Better World

Quantum healing codes are not only personal but also collective. When more individuals align with these frequencies, the ripple effect creates harmony on a larger scale. By living in harmony with the codes, you contribute to a collective field of healing and transformation.

Sharing the Codes with Others

Teach family, friends, and community members about quantum healing codes. Share your experiences and guide them in activating the codes that resonate with their needs. This practice strengthens collective well-being.

Using Codes in Group Meditations

Participate in or organize group meditations where participants focus on a specific quantum code, such as the "Peace Code." The combined intention amplifies the code's energy, creating a powerful impact on the collective consciousness.

Contributing to Global Healing

Apply codes to world events and challenges. For example, meditate on the "Healing Code" during natural disasters or the "Unity Code" in times of political division. While the effects may seem intangible, they contribute to the energetic fabric of the planet.

Long-Term Benefits of Quantum Healing Code Alignment

When you live in harmony with quantum healing codes, the benefits extend far beyond temporary healing. Over time, you will notice:

- Increased resilience to stress and challenges.
- Improved physical health and faster recovery from illness or injury.
- Greater emotional stability and inner peace.
- Deeper spiritual connection and intuitive guidance.
- Enhanced relationships and more meaningful connections.
- A stronger sense of purpose and fulfillment.

Practical Tips for Sustained Alignment

Regularly Refresh Your Knowledge

Revisit the codes periodically to deepen your understanding and refine your practice. As you grow, your relationship with the codes will evolve, revealing new layers of insight.

Stay Open to New Experiences

Quantum healing codes are dynamic. Stay curious and open to discovering new codes or applying existing ones in different ways. Trust your intuition to guide you.

Celebrate Your Progress

Living in harmony with the codes is a journey, not a destination. Celebrate the milestones along the way, whether it's overcoming a health challenge, deepening a relationship, or achieving a personal goal.

A Life in Harmony

Quantum healing codes are more than symbols or frequencies; they are an invitation to live a life of balance, vitality, and connection. By integrating these codes into your daily routine, relationships, and purpose, you align yourself with the infinite possibilities of the universe.

This harmony extends beyond the personal, creating ripples of healing that touch everyone and everything around you.

As you move forward, remember that living in harmony with quantum healing codes is not about perfection but presence. Every moment is an opportunity to reconnect, recalibrate, and realign with the frequencies that support your highest good.

You are the creator of your reality, and the codes are your guide. Live in their light, and watch as the world transforms.

Conclusion: Infinite Potential of Quantum Healing Codes

As we arrive at the conclusion of this journey into the world of Quantum Healing Codes, it is essential to reflect on the profound insights and transformative possibilities these codes offer.

Healing is not just about addressing symptoms; it is a journey of aligning with the universe's deepest truths, tapping into the energy that underpins all creation, and embracing the codes that guide us toward wholeness.

The essence of quantum healing lies in recognizing that we are not separate from the universe but rather an integral part of its vibrational dance.

Every cell, every thought, and every emotion resonates with the quantum field—a boundless, energetic matrix that holds the potential for infinite healing. The codes we have explored throughout this book are keys to accessing that potential.

A Universal Language for Transformation

Quantum Healing Codes are more than techniques or tools; they are a universal language, a vibrational blueprint that transcends time, space, and individual limitations.

These codes are not confined to any one discipline or belief system. Instead, they bridge science and spirituality, creating a harmonious union between the measurable and the mystical.

By engaging with these codes, you have learned to speak the language of energy. Whether through sound, light, visualization, or intention, you have discovered how to align yourself with frequencies that promote balance, peace, and vitality.

This alignment is not a one-time event but a lifelong dialogue—a continuous process of listening to your body, tuning your emotions, and recalibrating your energy to remain in harmony with the quantum field.

Empowerment Through Practice

Throughout this book, we've emphasized the practical application of quantum codes. Healing is not a passive experience; it is an active co-creation between you and the quantum realm.

By learning to identify the codes that resonate with your unique needs, you have become an empowered participant in your healing journey.

You now hold the tools to:

- Dissolve emotional blocks and release limiting beliefs.
- Rejuvenate your physical body by recalibrating cellular vibrations.
- Enhance spiritual connection and awaken higher states of consciousness.

The practice of using Quantum Healing Codes requires consistency, patience, and trust. There may be times when progress feels slow or obstacles seem insurmountable but remember that the universe is always responding.

Each activation, each intention, and each alignment moves you closer to a state of balance and well-being.

Healing the Whole and the Collective

One of the most profound realizations on this journey is that healing is not just personal—it is collective. As you heal, your energy shifts, creating ripples that influence those around you.

Quantum Healing Codes operate on frequencies that transcend individuality, making them a powerful tool for fostering unity and collective harmony.

When you align with the codes of love, compassion, and gratitude, you contribute to the healing of the planet. Imagine a world where millions of individuals consciously activate these frequencies, creating a collective vibration that promotes peace, understanding, and global well-being.

This is the true potential of Quantum Healing Codes: a bridge not only to personal transformation but to universal evolution.

A Journey Without End

Although this book comes to an end, your journey with Quantum Healing Codes is just beginning. The codes are infinite in their variations and applications. You may find new ways to personalize and adapt them as you grow. You may even discover entirely new codes that resonate uniquely with your evolving needs and aspirations.

This infinite potential is what makes quantum healing so extraordinary. There are no limits, no final destinations—only continuous expansion and deeper alignment with the quantum field.

Gratitude and Reflection

It is with deep gratitude that we conclude this exploration. Gratitude for the scientists, mystics, and healers who have paved the way for understanding quantum principles.

Gratitude for the universe, which has provided the codes and the energy that makes all healing possible. And gratitude for you, the reader, for embarking on this transformative journey.

Your willingness to explore, experiment, and embrace Quantum Healing Codes speaks to your courage and openness. Healing is not always easy, but it is one of the most rewarding paths you can walk.

By engaging with these codes, you have taken a powerful step toward realizing your full potential and contributing to the greater good.

An Invitation to Share

As you move forward, consider sharing the gift of Quantum Healing Codes with others. Healing, like love, multiplies when shared. Whether you use these codes to help loved ones, teach them to others, or integrate them into your professional practice, you become a channel for transformation.

The world is in great need of healing—on physical, emotional, and spiritual levels. By sharing what you have learned, you can be a beacon of light, a guide, and a healer in your community.

Final Thoughts

The power of Quantum Healing Codes lies not in the codes themselves but in the resonance they awaken within you. Healing is not something external that you receive; it is an inner truth that you remember.

The codes are simply guides—reminders of the wholeness that has always existed within you.

As you close this book, take a moment to sit in silence. Feel the energy of the quantum field around you and within you. Trust that you have everything you need to heal, grow, and thrive.

In the words of the quantum field: You are whole. You are connected. You are infinite.

Go forth with this knowledge, and may the codes guide you to a life of health, joy, and profound harmony.

With infinite gratitude,

Ecnal Ver

Glossary of Terms

Alignment

The state of being energetically balanced and in harmony with the natural flow of universal energy. Alignment is essential for effectively utilizing quantum healing codes.

Ascension Codes

Advanced healing codes designed to support spiritual awakening and higher states of consciousness.

Biofield

The energetic field surrounding and permeating the human body. This field, also known as the aura, interacts with quantum codes to influence health and well-being.

Cellular Memory

The concept that cells retain information about past experiences and traumas. Quantum healing codes can rewrite cellular memory for improved health.

Chakra

Energy centers within the body that regulate the flow of vital energy (prana). Quantum healing codes can help balance and activate chakras for optimal health.

Chakra Activation Codes

Specialized codes designed to open, balance, and harmonize specific chakras. These codes enhance the flow of energy through the body's energy centers.

Coherence

The state of synchronization and harmony within energy systems. Quantum healing codes foster coherence between mind, body, and spirit.

Consciousness

The awareness and perception of oneself and the surrounding universe. It plays a critical role in activating and aligning with quantum healing codes.

DNA Activation

The process of unlocking dormant genetic potential for healing and transformation. Some quantum healing codes are designed specifically for DNA activation.

Emotional Codes

Specific quantum healing codes designed to release trapped emotions and foster emotional balance. These codes address deep-seated emotional wounds and trauma.

Energetic Blueprint

The unique vibrational signature of an individual, which determines their physical, emotional, and spiritual health. Quantum healing codes can recalibrate the energetic blueprint to restore balance.

Energetic Imprints

Residual energy patterns left by thoughts, emotions, or experiences. Quantum healing codes can clear or reprogram these imprints.

Energy Matrix

The interconnected network of energy fields that make up reality. Quantum healing codes operate within this matrix to create systemic change.

Energy Signature

The unique vibrational pattern of an individual, object, or situation. Quantum healing codes interact with energy signatures to create specific outcomes.

Frequency

The rate at which a vibration or wave oscillates. Each quantum healing code corresponds to a specific frequency that influences health and consciousness.

Grounding

A practice of connecting with the Earth's energy to stabilize and balance one's energy field. Grounding enhances the effectiveness of quantum healing codes.

Harmonic Frequencies

Frequencies that naturally resonate with each other, creating a state of balance and beauty. Quantum healing codes often align with harmonic frequencies for maximum effect.

Healing Codes

Energetic patterns or sequences of vibrations that communicate directly with the body's energy systems to promote healing. These codes are the central focus of this book.

Holographic Healing

The concept that the body, mind, and spirit are interconnected and can be healed as a whole system. Quantum healing codes function holographically to address multiple dimensions of being.

Infinite Potential

The limitless possibilities inherent in the quantum field. Quantum healing codes tap into this potential to create profound transformation.

Intention

The focused energy of thought and emotion directed toward a specific goal or outcome. Intention enhances the effectiveness of quantum healing codes.

Intuitive Guidance

Insights and messages received from higher consciousness or inner knowing. Intuition helps individuals identify the right quantum healing codes for their needs.

Light Codes

Specific sequences of light frequencies that activate healing processes in the body. Light codes are often integrated with quantum healing codes for enhanced results.

Manifestation Codes

Quantum healing codes designed to align energy with desired outcomes, such as health, abundance, or peace.

Meditation

A practice of focused attention and mindfulness used to quiet the mind and connect with higher frequencies. Meditation is a tool for activating and aligning with quantum healing codes.

Morphogenetic Field

The blueprint-like field that guides the development and structure of living organisms. Quantum healing codes interact with this field to influence health and repair.

Neuroplasticity

The brain's ability to reorganize and adapt by forming new neural connections. Quantum healing codes can influence neuroplasticity to create positive mental and emotional shifts.

Photon

A particle of light that carries electromagnetic energy. Photons are used in light codes to deliver healing frequencies.

Placebo Effect

The phenomenon where belief in a treatment leads to healing outcomes, regardless of the treatment's inherent properties. Quantum healing codes amplify this effect through focused intention and resonance.

Prana

The life force energy that flows through all living beings. Quantum healing codes enhance and balance prana to restore vitality.

Quantum Field

An all-encompassing field of energy that connects every particle in the universe. Quantum healing codes operate within this field to influence health and reality.

Quantum Frequencies

Specific vibrational patterns derived from quantum physics, used to create healing codes. These frequencies resonate with the body's energy systems to promote healing.

Quantum Healing

A method of healing that involves manipulating energy fields and consciousness to create changes in the physical, emotional, and spiritual states of being.

Quantum Reprogramming

The process of using quantum healing codes to overwrite old patterns and introduce new, healthier ones.

Resonance

The phenomenon where one energy system vibrates in harmony with another. Quantum healing codes use resonance to align the body's energy systems with optimal frequencies.

Sacred Geometry

The study of shapes and patterns that have symbolic and energetic significance. Many quantum healing codes are derived from sacred geometric principles.

Scalar Energy

A form of subtle energy that exists in the quantum field and has healing properties. Quantum healing codes can tap into scalar energy to enhance their effects.

Self-Healing

The innate ability of the body and mind to repair and restore themselves. Quantum healing codes activate and amplify self-healing processes.

Solfeggio Frequencies

Specific sound frequencies believed to promote healing and spiritual growth. These frequencies are often integrated into quantum healing codes.

Sound Codes

Sequences of specific sound vibrations used to activate healing processes. Quantum healing codes often incorporate sound codes for deeper resonance.

Subtle Energy

Energy that is not yet measurable by conventional scientific instruments but has significant effects on health and consciousness. Quantum healing codes work with subtle energy fields.

Synergy

The combined effect of multiple elements working together to produce a result greater than the sum of their individual effects. Quantum healing codes create synergy by combining intention, light, and sound.

Thought Forms

Energetic patterns created by focused thoughts. Positive thought forms can amplify the power of quantum healing codes.

Torsion Field

A subtle energy field created by the twisting of space-time. Torsion fields are believed to store and transmit information, playing a role in how quantum healing codes function.

Universal Energy

The limitless energy that permeates the universe and sustains all life. Quantum healing codes draw from this source to effect change and transformation.

Vibration

The oscillation of energy within a particular frequency range. Quantum healing codes operate by attuning the body to specific healing vibrations.

Visualization

The practice of imagining desired outcomes to align energy and consciousness. Visualization is a key tool for activating quantum healing codes.

Wave-Particle Duality

The quantum phenomenon where particles such as photons exhibit both wave-like and particle-like behavior. This principle underpins the workings of quantum healing codes.

Zero-Point Energy

The lowest possible energy state of a quantum system, representing infinite potential. Quantum healing codes often tap into zero-point energy to unlock new possibilities for healing.

Quantum Healing Codes:
Sound & Light Wave Metrics

Code for Balance

Sound Frequency: 432 Hz (Known as the frequency of the universe, it promotes natural harmony and balance).

Light Wave: Green (The color of healing and equilibrium, green connects the mind and body).

Use for: Relieving stress, grounding chaotic energy, and restoring inner peace.

How to Apply: Play 432 Hz music or soundscapes while visualizing a soft green light enveloping your body. Practice slow, mindful breathing to amplify its effects.

Code for Emotional Release

Sound Frequency: 396 Hz (Targets and dissolves guilt, fear, and deep emotional blocks).

Light Wave: Orange (Symbolizes emotional energy, creativity, and the flow of life).

Use for: Letting go of grief, releasing suppressed anger, and unblocking emotions.

How to Apply: Use a 396 Hz tuning fork or sound track alongside meditation. Visualize an orange light flowing through your sacral chakra to release pent-up emotions.

Code for Physical Healing

Sound Frequency: 528 Hz (Known as the "Miracle Tone," it is believed to repair DNA and regenerate cells).

Light Wave: Blue (Calming and soothing, blue reduces inflammation and promotes relaxation).

Use for: Healing physical injuries, easing pain, and improving cellular health.

How to Apply: Play 528 Hz frequencies during rest or healing rituals. Pair with blue light therapy or visualization techniques to strengthen its impact.

Code for Spiritual Awakening

Sound Frequency: 963 Hz (Activates the pineal gland and deepens connection with higher consciousness).

Light Wave: Violet (The color of spiritual energy and transformation, violet enhances intuition).

Use for: Expanding spiritual awareness, awakening intuition, and connecting to universal energy.

How to Apply: Meditate with 963 Hz music, imagining a violet beam of light entering through your crown chakra and radiating through your body.

Code for DNA Activation

Sound Frequency: 528 Hz (The "DNA Repair" frequency, said to unlock dormant genetic potential).

Light Wave: Gold (Represents transformation, regeneration, and vitality).

Use for: Enhancing energy levels, optimizing health, and activating latent DNA codes.

How to Apply: Play 528 Hz tones during physical or mental exercises. Visualize golden light spiraling through your cells, repairing and strengthening them.

Code for Chakra Balancing

Sound Frequency: 7 Chakra Tones (Root: 256 Hz, Sacral: 288 Hz, Solar Plexus: 320 Hz, Heart: 341 Hz, Throat: 384 Hz, Third Eye: 426 Hz, Crown: 480 Hz).

Light Wave: Rainbow (A spectrum of colors that align with each chakra for total balance).

Use for: Aligning all energy centers, enhancing well-being, and removing blockages.

How to Apply: Work through each chakra sequentially using corresponding tones and colors. Visualize a rainbow of light flowing through your body from root to crown.

Code for Manifestation

Sound Frequency: 741 Hz (Clears creative blocks and amplifies manifestation energy).

Light Wave: Yellow (Associated with focus, willpower, and the energy of creation).

Use for: Attracting abundance, achieving goals, and manifesting intentions.

How to Apply: Use 741 Hz tones during visualization exercises. Picture a vibrant yellow light surrounding you as you focus on your desired outcome.

Code for Protection

Sound Frequency: 417 Hz (Cleanses negativity and enhances resilience).

Light Wave: Indigo (Shields the aura and deflects negative energy).

Use for: Establishing energetic boundaries and shielding from harmful influences.

How to Apply: Combine 417 Hz music with visualization of indigo light forming a protective barrier around you. Repeat affirmations to strengthen your energetic shield.

Code for Vitality

Sound Frequency: 285 Hz (Rejuvenates energy fields and promotes physical restoration).

Light Wave: Red (Stimulates vitality, strength, and energy flow).

Use for: Boosting energy levels, overcoming fatigue, and enhancing stamina.

How to Apply: Play 285 Hz tones while engaging in movement-based activities. Envision red light energizing your entire being.

Code for Sleep and Relaxation

Sound Frequency: 174 Hz (Promotes deep relaxation and pain relief).

Light Wave: Soft Blue (Encourages tranquility and rest).

Use for: Overcoming insomnia, relieving tension, and achieving deep sleep.

How to Apply: Use 174 Hz tones as bedtime background music. Dim the lights and imagine a soft blue glow enveloping you.

Code for Creativity

Sound Frequency: 639 Hz (Facilitates harmony in relationships and sparks inspiration).

Light Wave: Orange (Enhances creative flow and emotional connection).

Use for: Unlocking new ideas, fostering innovation, and strengthening creative expression.

How to Apply: Play 639 Hz frequencies while brainstorming or creating. Imagine orange light pulsing through your sacral chakra.

Code for Heart Healing

Sound Frequency: 341 Hz (Aligns with the heart chakra for emotional healing).

Light Wave: Pink (Symbolizes love, compassion, and forgiveness).

Use for: Healing emotional trauma, fostering love, and building connection.

How to Apply: Meditate with pink light and soothing 341 Hz tones. Focus on the heart center, releasing pain and welcoming love.

Code for Focus and Clarity

Sound Frequency: 741 Hz (Sharpens mental focus and clears distractions).

Light Wave: Yellow (Enhances concentration and mental clarity).

Use for: Studying, decision-making, and solving complex problems.

How to Apply: Use 741 Hz frequencies while working or meditating. Visualize a bright yellow sphere illuminating your mind.

Code for Immune Support

Sound Frequency: 285 Hz (Enhances physical resilience and cellular repair).

Light Wave: Green (Boosts immune strength and vitality).

Use for: Strengthening immunity, speeding up recovery, and maintaining health.

How to Apply: Play 285 Hz music while visualizing green light surrounding and strengthening your body.

Code for Harmony

Sound Frequency: 852 Hz (Promotes mental clarity and spiritual harmony).

Light Wave: White (Balances and integrates all energies).

Use for: Resolving conflicts, fostering peace, and achieving inner balance.

How to Apply: Use 852 Hz tones with deep breathing exercises. Visualize white light spreading through your environment and relationships.

This expanded reference integrates sound and light frequencies, offering detailed applications for each Quantum Healing Code.

These codes harness specific vibrations to promote balance, healing, and transformation.

ECNAL VER

About the Author

The *Quantum Potential* series by Quantum Potential Publishing invites readers to discover a transformative intersection of faith, science, and personal growth.

These books are a series that illuminates how quantum principles can empower us to live with purpose, connection, and limitless possibility.

Each book builds on quantum physics applied in our lives, offering a holistic approach to living a life full of love, healing, and transformation.

To learn more and connect with a community embracing these principles, visit:

QuantumPotential.com

Book Series on Amazon.com

Unlock *your* quantum potential, and step into a reality rich with infinite possibilities.

Made in the USA
Las Vegas, NV
31 January 2025

17273352R00075